The Amazing Egg Book

Written by
Margaret Griffin
and **Deborah Seed**

Illustrated by
Linda Hendry

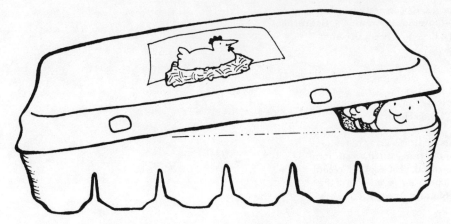

▲
▼▼
Addison-Wesley Publishing Company, Inc.
Reading, Massachusetts   Menlo Park, California   New York
Don Mills, Ontario   Wokingham, England   Amsterdam
Bonn   Sydney   Singapore   Tokyo   Madrid   San Juan

Acknowledgements

We would like to thank our four children — Alexander and Dina, Thomas and Catherine — for their help in testing much of the material, as well as Martin Reyto and John Weldon for their support. We are similarly indebted to Val Wyatt, who proved to be a first-rate editor, and Laurie Wark at Kids Can Press. Three officers at The Ontario Egg Producers' Marketing Board provided invaluable advice regarding recipes and egg production: Leslie Ballentine, Communications Officer; Theresa Miller, Advertising and Promotion Manager; and Ellen Badeski, Consumer Adviser. We are also grateful to the following for aiding us in our research: John Ruttner of Toronto, Dr. D.R. Griffin of Princeton, New Jersey; Ruth C. Griffin of Boston; Marcella Weiershausen of Fredericksburg, Texas; C.I. Petros and David Lewis of Montreal; and the Resource Centre at Champlain Regional College, St. Lambert, Quebec.

Library of Congress Cataloging-in-Publication Data

Griffin, Margaret, 1948–
    The amazing egg book / written by Margaret Griffin and Deborah Seed ; illustrated by Linda Hendry.
        p. cm.
    Summary: Discusses where eggs come from, what functions they serve, and how they can be used for food or decoration.
    ISBN 0-201-52334-5
    1. Eggs — Juvenile literature.   2. Egg decoration — Juvenile literature.   3. Eggshell craft — Juvenile literature.   4. Egg carton craft — Juvenile literature.   [1. Eggs.]   I. Seed, Deborah.
    II. Hendry, Linda, ill.   III. Title.
    QL956.5.G75   1990
    745.594′4 — dc20   89-28071
                                                                    CIP

Edited by Valerie Wyatt
Book design by Michael Solomon
Cover design by Copenhaver Cumpston
Cover photograph by Marshall Henrichs
Set in 13-point Century Schoolbook by Alphabets, Canada

ABCDEFGHIJ–AL–89
First printing, January 1990

Contents

1. How the world began 6
   Eggs to grow on 8
   Say it with eggs 10
   Make your own dyes 12

2. Why do eggs exist? 14
   Go lay an egg ... in the ocean 16
   Amazing egg layers 18
   Go lay an egg ... on land 20
   Types of birds' eggs 24
   Master builders 26
   Egg Olympics 28

3. Eating eggs 30
   Eggs to the rescue 32
   Strange-but-true egg food 34

4. The egg up close 38
   How strong is an eggshell? 42
   The disappearing eggshell 44
   Inside the egg 46
   Making an egg 48
   From the farm to you 50

5. Egg fun 54
   Three great egg-carton games 56
   Egg art 59

Glossary 62
Index 63
Answers 64

What do sea horses, flamingos, spiders, bumblebees, octopuses, frogs and robins have in common? They all lay eggs.

Eggs come in a variety of sizes and shapes, colours and textures. Insect eggs can be so tiny you'd need a microscope to see them. Hummingbird eggs are about the size of jelly beans, while ostrich eggs are as large as footballs. Snake eggs are soft and leathery, but bird eggs are hard and brittle. Sea creatures produce millions of eggs at a time; some birds produce only one egg every other year.

This book is about all the different kinds of eggs. It's about eggs as homes for the creatures inside them, about the

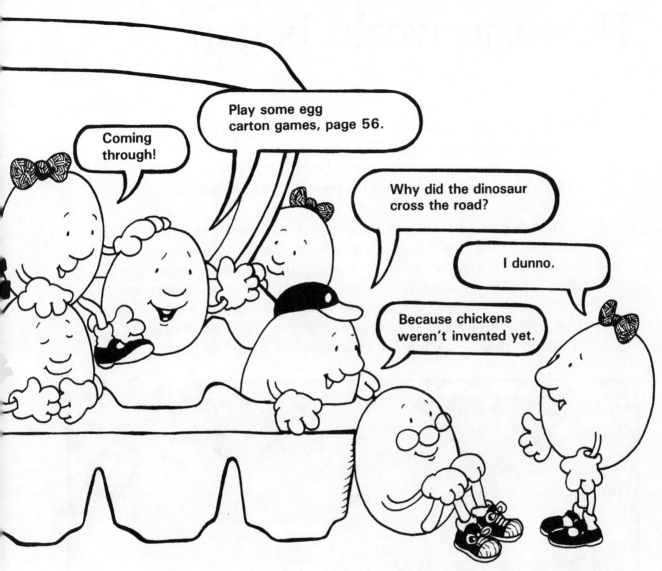

different ways the parents care for them and about the eggs you eat. Read *The Amazing Egg Book* and you'll:

- discover tales and legends people tell about eggs
- learn some magic tricks, such as how to make an eggshell disappear
- decorate eggshells
- find out how to turn an egg carton into a game board
- try out some delicious egg recipes.

P.S. Whenever you see an egg word that you don't understand, check the glossary at the back of the book.

1. How the world began

Ancient people watched in wonder as living creatures struggled out of their eggs. The eggs looked lifeless, like stones, but then suddenly out climbed birds, turtles, even snakes or crocodiles. No wonder people thought that the whole world had hatched from an egg, too.

Here is one very ancient Hindu myth from India that tells how the whole world began with an egg. In the beginning, before the world was made, it was completely dark. There were no animals or people. There was nothing at all. When the Lord Creator, called Brahma, was ready to form the world, he first made the waters. The waters heated up and produced Hiranyagarbha, a golden egg that shone like the sun itself.

Brahma stayed in the egg for a year until his thoughts split the egg in two. The bottom half of the shell became the earth, and the upper half became the sky. The outer membrane of the egg formed the mountains. The inner membrane turned into the clouds and mists. What had been the veins became the rivers, and what had been the fluid became the seas.

There were many other egg myths about how the world was formed. For example, in the South Pacific, the Samoans wondered where their islands had come from. The Heavenly One, they believed, had lived for a while in an egg. Finally he broke it into pieces, bit by bit, and flung the pieces over the water. Those pieces became the Samoan Islands.

Ancient Egyptians believed that the universe, when it was new, was silent. The silence was broken by the cackle of a heavenly goose as it laid the world egg on a mound of mud. That egg contained Ra, the Sun god, who rose every morning and set every evening.

The Maoris, the native people of New Zealand, believed their ancestors came from an egg, too. They say that a bird dropped an egg on the empty sea. When the egg burst open, guess what came out? A man and a woman, a boy and a girl, a dog and a pig, and a canoe. Everyone then hopped into the canoe, and it eventually drifted over to New Zealand.

If *you* had to invent an egg myth to explain the world, what would you come up with?

Did you know that...

- Egyptians wore egg-shaped amulets to give them magical protection and power? To them, the egg symbolized the idea of rebirth in the next life.
- many ancient tombs in Russia and Sweden contained clay eggs? The Romans placed eggs in graves along with dead bodies, too.

Eggs to grow on

People have long been fascinated by eggs. For more than two thousand years eggs have been important symbols of birth and growth, or fertility. For example, long ago at ploughing time, European farmers carried eggs into the fields, hoping that the eggs would double or triple the crops they were planting. Here are some other ways eggs were used....

Buried Treasure

Ukrainian farmers buried special krashanka eggs in the hope that this treasure would bring good weather and plentiful crops. Before they were planted, these eggs were dyed a solid colour, then rolled in green oats. Krashanka eggs were considered especially powerful because they were thought to cure sick people, who wore them around their necks.

Here Comes the Bride

If you were a bride in France four hundred years ago, you had to break an egg on the floor when you entered your new home to make sure you would have children. Married couples in the Ukraine received eggs, too, if they didn't have any children. Future mothers were given eggs decorated with chickens. Future fathers got eggs decorated with roosters!

Eggs for Luck

What gift would you give to a new-born baby — a stuffed animal or toy? Not too long ago in England, babies would receive an egg, some bread and a sixpence. These charms ensured that the babies would never go hungry or be poor.

Egg on Your Face!

Nowadays we say a person has egg on his face if he does something that he's embarrassed by. Years ago in Albania, people broke an egg over a baby's face to protect him or her from the Evil Eye. Mothers of boys were given an even number of eggs; mothers of girls received an odd number.

Superstitions to Tell Your Friends

Over the years, people have believed in many different superstitions related to eggs. Here are a few to tell your friends.

- If you have a stomach-ache, try to find some eggs that were laid on a Friday. These eggs will cure stomach-aches. But never buy *hens* that hatch from eggs laid on Friday! They will be too tough to eat.

- Eggs laid on Good Friday, two days before Easter Sunday, are extra special. They can protect your house from being struck by lightning.

- After you boil eggs, be sure to get rid of the water. If you wash your hands in it, some people think you might get warts. (This is just a superstition, remember.)

- Ukrainian farmers believed so strongly in the power of eggs that some thought eggs could protect them from fire. If a house did catch fire, someone would carry an egg around the burning area so that the blaze would not spread any further.

- To avoid bad luck, turn the shells from soft-boiled eggs upside down and smash them. Why? Years ago people believed that witches needed unbroken shells to concoct their magic spells or used them as boats and flying vessels. People also broke their eggshells because they were afraid a shell left intact could cause a shipwreck.

Say it with eggs

Exchanging gifts of eggs is a tradition for marking the coming of spring. Parsis (Persians who now live in Iran) believed the world hatched from an egg during the spring equinox, one of the two days of the year when the hours of daylight and night are the same. They celebrate their New Year around March 21 by cooking special food and giving one another coloured eggs. Ancient Greeks and Romans exchanged coloured eggs at spring festivals, too, just as Christians now give their children decorated or chocolate eggs at Easter.

Passover

A hard-boiled egg is always part of the special food prepared for Passover, an important Jewish festival. Each spring, shortly after the equinox, Jews celebrate Passover to remind them of the time when their Hebrew ancestors fled from Egypt over 5700 years ago.

On the first two nights of the holiday, the family gathers for a meal called a Seder, meaning "order." On the Seder plate

Boiling Bunny Eggs

If Santa's toys are made at the North Pole, where does the Easter rabbit boil all its eggs? In Fredericksburg, Texas, or that's how the story goes.

Around 1848 on Easter eve, some Comanche Indians built fires near Fredericksburg to send smoke signals to one another if a peace treaty were signed with the settlers. The children of one settler wanted to know why the fires were burning. Their mother replied that the rabbits were boiling Easter eggs! Nowadays the Boy Scouts and townspeople tend the fires each Easter.

are arranged several symbolic foods: a roasted lamb bone, green vegetables, horseradish to represent bitter herbs, charoset (grated apples and nuts) and three pieces of matzo (flat, cracker-like bread), and an egg. The egg isn't eaten because it symbolizes fertility and hope.

Easter

For Christians, Easter is an important festival because it celebrates the miracle of Christ coming back to life after he was crucified. Traditionally, eggs were dyed red at Easter to remind Christians that Christ shed his blood for them. According to one Rumanian legend, the first Easter eggs were dyed red because Mary, Christ's mother, placed them in a basket below the cross, and his blood dripped over them.

Extraordinary Easter Customs

- For some Christians the egg is also a symbol of the stone that mysteriously rolled away from the door of the tomb where Christ was buried. In Scotland, children roll their decorated eggs down a slope. The owner of the fastest egg gets to keep the other eggs. If you set up such a contest this year, make sure to use hard-boiled eggs!
- At the cathedral in Chester, England, the bishop and dean used to toss an egg back and forth with the choir boys during the Easter service. So many eggs were smashed that the participants eventually switched to balls instead.
- According to the *Guinness Book of World Records*, the largest egg hunt in the world took place in 1986, at the home of the Garrison family in Homer, Georgia. More than 10 000 people searched for 72 000 hard-boiled eggs and 40 000 candy eggs.

Make your own dyes

You can dye eggs by boiling them with onion skins, dandelion flowers, spinach, beets, blueberries and strawberries or even grape juice. Here's how to get three colours from one cabbage.

You'll need:

1 saucepan (not aluminum)
3 clear plastic glasses or jars
coffee sticks or spoons
500 mL shredded red cabbage   2 cups
vinegar or lemon juice
2 mL baking soda   ½ tsp

1. Put the cabbage in the pan and add enough water to cover the pieces. Put on the lid and bring the water to a boil over medium heat. Reduce the heat and let the mixture simmer for half an hour. Let the pan cool.
2. Divide the cabbage liquid evenly among the three glasses.

3. Slowly add a few drops of vinegar or lemon to one glass — one drop at a time. What happens? Adding vinegar or lemon makes the solution more acidic.
4. Sprinkle the baking soda into the second glass of cabbage water. The baking soda makes the water more alkaline, or less acidic. What colour do you get this time?

To make your eggs look marbled, wrap the egg with shredded cabbage in a piece of cheesecloth and fasten. Boil this package in clear water for about 10 minutes. If you want green spots, sprinkle on some baking soda before unwrapping the egg. To make it shine, wipe with vegetable oil.

Ukrainian Eggs

Ukrainian Easter eggs, called pysanky (pih SAN kee), are famous because of their beautiful designs and colours. The eggs were blessed in church at Easter and then given to friends on Easter Sunday. People kept them as good luck charms for years.

Decorating psyanky eggs is like designing batiks on material. The intricate design is built up gradually, using different dyes and layers of wax. Traditional craftspeople use a special writing instrument, called a kystka, to sketch on the designs in hot wax.

You can try this traditional craft, too, by using hard-boiled eggs, a white crayon and some natural or fabric dyes. Try some of the designs on this page. Use both light and dark colours of dye.

1. Use the crayon to draw your design around the entire egg, from top to bottom and around the middle. Whatever you crayon will stay white.

2. Dip the egg in the lightest dye and let it dry. Crayon over the sections you want to stay that colour. Repeat, using darker dyes each time.

3. Dip the egg in hot water to remove the crayon wax. With a grown-up's help, you can also hold the egg beside the flame of a candle until the wax melts, then wipe off the melted wax in paper towel.

2. Why do eggs exist?

No creature can live forever, so each species has to be able to reproduce — to create more of its own kind. Simple one-celled animals such as planarians (flatworms), found in ponds, can reproduce by splitting in two. Instead of one organism, two new ones are created, which are exactly alike. When life first evolved on our planet, this was the only way creatures could reproduce. This process is called asexual reproduction, or reproduction without sex.

As more complex plants and animals evolved over thousands and millions of years, a second form of reproduction developed. This process is called sexual reproduction because it needs two parents. The female provides an egg (or ovum) and the male supplies the sperm.

This egg must usually be fertilized by sperm before it can begin to grow. After fertilization, an amazing process takes place inside the egg. New cells start growing at a tremendous speed to make an embryo (EM bree oh). This embryo will grow into a new creature.

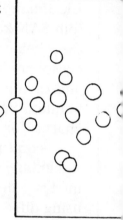

The first eggs were laid in the ocean because that's where their parents lived. The eggs we find in the ocean today are like the ones laid millions of years ago. They are often very tiny and soft, and don't contain enough egg food, or yolk, to let the embryos develop fully before they hatch. The embryos of many ocean animals emerge as partly developed creatures called larvae, which must eat a great deal to grow to their full size and shape.

As evolution continued, some species started to move out of the water and began to live on land. But they still had to return to the water to lay their eggs because without water, the eggs would dry out and never hatch.

Then a new type of egg developed that let land animals lay their eggs far from water. This egg had a shell and membranes that held the water in and kept the egg from drying out. Often it also contained enough food so that the embryo could grow

Many sea animals, like these brine shrimp, start ou as eggs and hatch as larvae before becomin adults.

and hatch fully formed. It was a safe watery home for the tiny developing animal inside.

Sea creatures and other early animals such as amphibians, reptiles, birds and insects all laid their eggs *outside* their bodies. But gradually a new kind of animal — mammals — evolved. They kept the embryo *inside* the mother's body where it could be well protected and nourished until the baby was born.

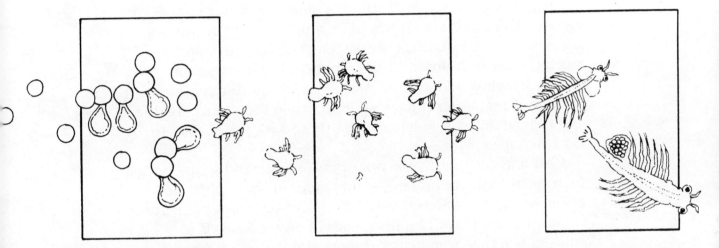

Exceptional Eggs

Did you know that...

- two mammals in Australia — the duckbilled platypus and the spiny anteater — lay eggs? When the babies hatch, they lap up their mother's milk, just like other mammal babies do.

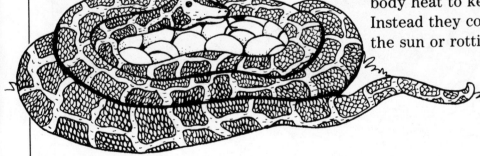

- an earthworm can produce both eggs *and* sperm? Two worms trade sperm so that each worm's eggs get fertilized by the sperm of the other worm. The thick band around the worm makes a cocoon or egg sac for the eggs.
- the python incubates its eggs by wrapping itself around them? Most cold-blooded animals can't rely on their body heat to keep the eggs warm. Instead they count on the heat from the sun or rotting vegetation.

Go lay an egg...in the ocean

If you were going to lay an egg, where would you want to lay it?

In the ocean? You'd certainly be in good company alongside the sponges and corals, oysters and clams, lobsters and shrimp, and all the millions of fish. The ocean provides all the things a developing egg needs. First, there's plenty of water so that the egg won't dry out, which would be a problem if you were to lay it on land. Second, the water temperature stays pretty much the same; it doesn't suddenly heat up or drop to a freeze, which would kill the egg. Third, the water contains oxygen and minerals for the embryo inside the egg to breathe and to feed on as it develops. And there's plenty of food to eat when it hatches.

Most animals that live in water lay smaller and simpler eggs than those that live on land — and more of them. Fish, for example, lay thousands, even millions, of eggs at a time. The common mussel lays 12 million eggs in one session. If a chicken laid that many eggs, they would cover a football field.

How does a mother mussel sit on all these eggs at once? She

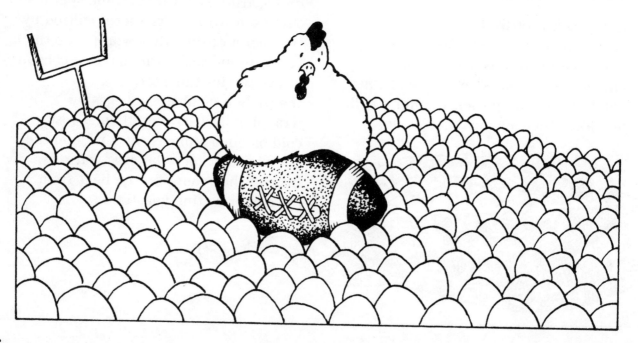

Other Wet Places

Ponds, streams and puddles are filled
with all sorts of eggs laid by fish,
amphibians, and insects. Here are a
few wet places where these creatures
lay their eggs.

in swamps	dragonflies, frogs
on wet cave walls	salamanders
in puddles	whirligig beetles
in rushing creeks	speckled trout
under rotten logs	great grey slugs
under wet stones	some types of toads
in pails of water	mosquitoes
in damp soil	earthworms
under lily pads	snails

doesn't even *try* to take care of her eggs. After she sheds
them in the water, the male releases sperm that fertilizes
them. The eggs float around, unprotected by the parents, until
they are ready to hatch. Ninety-nine percent are likely to get
eaten.

Fish need to lay millions of eggs because so many hungry
predators are waiting to gobble them up. But even though fish
don't usually stay around to care for their eggs, the fate of the
eggs isn't entirely left up to chance. Many fish have instincts
that make them lay eggs in a place where the eggs are more
likely to survive.

For example, a safe time to lay eggs in the ocean is at night
when greedy predators are asleep. Fish that lay their eggs at
night are attracted to the upper levels by the moonlight
shining down through the water and food near the surface.
Other species of fish lay eggs equipped with floats — small
drops of oil that make them rise to the surface. Another safe
place to lay eggs is near currents or outgoing tides, which
carry them far away from crowded neighbourhoods full of
hungry predators. The young fish return home when they are
better able to defend themselves against danger.

Amazing egg layers

Some creatures that lay eggs in water have developed special ways to make sure that the eggs hatch safely.

Hanging Out the Eggs

Most sea creatures simply shed their eggs and leave. But not the mother octopus. She's one of the best mothers in the ocean. She lays up to 150 000 tiny, oval eggs at a time, twisting them together into long strings. Then she hangs them up like laundry from the ceiling of her underwater cave. During the next six weeks she keeps them clean by waving her tentacles through the strands and blowing jets of water on them.

Bubble Nests

Usually, after an animal has built a nest, the mother climbs inside to lay her eggs. Not the paradise fish! She lays her eggs *underneath* the nest, which her mate has built for her. The nest is a mass of sticky bubbles shaped like an upside-down bowl, and it floats on the surface of the water. Each egg contains a large droplet of oil that makes the egg bob up right into the nest. If any eggs float away from the nest, the father catches them in his mouth and spits them back home.

A Pregnant Male?

The male sea horse has a pouch on his abdomen much like that of the kangaroo. The female lays between 250 to 600 eggs inside the male's pouch using an ovipositor, or egg-laying tube. The eggs are fertilized as they pass into the pouch. As the babies get bigger and bigger, so does the father's stomach.

Floating Greenhouses

Frogs lay their eggs in ponds and lakes — a thousand at a time. The tiny eggs have a gooey, jelly-like covering that swells up as soon as the eggs get wet. The pile of jelly, called spawn, is like a greenhouse: it helps to keep the eggs warm by absorbing and holding the heat from the sun. It also keeps them safe from predators, who don't like the taste.

Biggest Egg Layer in the Sea

The American oyster takes the prize for laying the most eggs. It sheds 500 million eggs a year. The most eggs laid by the best egg-laying chicken one year was a measly 371 eggs.

Go lay an egg...on land

What would you need if you decided to lay an egg on land? You'd want a container that wouldn't leak too much to prevent the egg from drying out. You'd also want some way to protect the insides from getting punctured and to save the creature inside from bumps and bruises. The shell and membranes of an egg do these very jobs.

Land animals have different ways of ensuring that their eggs hatch safely. Some take great care to protect the eggs from predators. The male midwife toad, for example, sticks his eggs to his legs and hops around as usual until they hatch. Other egg layers don't wait around until their eggs hatch. Instead they provide their eggs with camouflage colours so that they blend in with their surroundings. Many snakes hide their eggs under stones or leaves, and turtles bury their eggs. Snake and turtle eggs are white; they don't need a shell camouflage because they're hidden or buried. Here's how some other clever parents take care of *their* eggs.

Spider Sitters

If you've read *Charlotte's Web*, you'll know how spiders take care of their eggs. They build special egg sacs out of the same silk that they use to spin their webs. Some carry the egg sacs under their bodies until the baby spiders hatch. Sometimes the egg sacs are so huge they have to walk on tiptoe! Other kinds of spiders hang the egg sacs on their webs. Look for them on old fences or between plant stems.

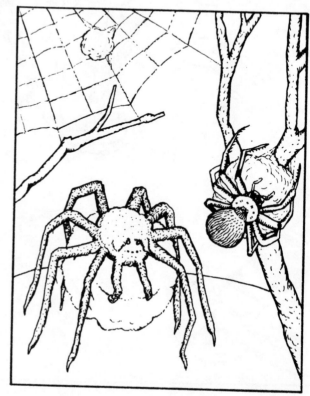

Happy Father's Day

Some animal fathers deserve a medal for egg watching. In South America, the male rhea, a large bird like the ostrich, builds a nest for five or six females. The females take turns laying eggs in the nest until it's full, then the male chases the females away and guards the eggs by himself. Sometimes there can be over 50 eggs.

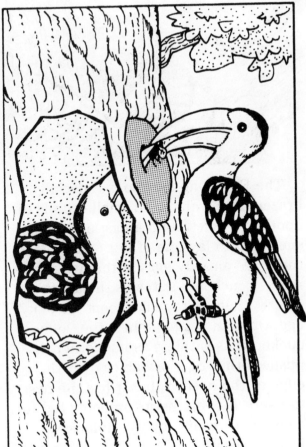

Mom and Pop Team

Many birds work together to build the nest, incubate the eggs and feed the babies. Hornbills have a very unusual mom-and-pop act. The female hornbill builds her nest in a tree hole, then seals herself inside with the eggs. During the long incubation period, the male feeds his mate through a small slit in the door. Sometimes that opening is so tiny that only the tip of her tongue can poke through!

After the eggs hatch, the mother breaks down the door and goes out to help the father gather food. The young quickly rebuild the mud door and let their parents wait on them a bit longer. Sometimes they disagree when it's time to leave the nest. The older ones may start trying to tear down the wall while the younger ones desperately try to repair it!

Eggsitters Wanted!

Caring for eggs can be a time-consuming and tiring job. Some animal parents, like birds, share the job. Others may get an entirely different species to help out. That kind of co-operation is called symbiosis.

Some kinds of ants and aphids help each other out in several ways. The aphids produce a sweet syrup, called honeydew, which the ants love to drink. Ants raise aphids to provide them with their favourite drink the same way farmers raise cows to provide us with milk. The ants protect the aphids from predators. In winter, the ants carry the aphids' eggs into their own nests and tend them until spring. After the aphids hatch, the ants carry them back outside, placing them carefully on the plants that aphids love to eat.

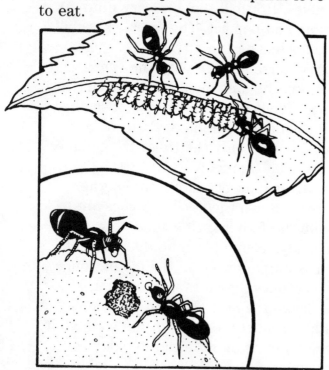

Tricksters

Sometimes one kind of animal tricks another kind of animal into taking care of its eggs. This is how an African fly fools the ferocious Driver ant. The fly waits until she sees a whole line of ants marching back to their nest. If one of the ants is empty-handed, she drops her packet of eggs right in front of it. The ant automatically scoops up the packet and carries it into the anthill where there will be a plentiful supply of food for the baby flies when they hatch.

The European cuckoo is especially brazen. She waits until smaller birds of another species build a nest and then sneaks in to lay one of her own eggs. If there are already eggs in the nest, the mother cuckoo just tosses them out — or eats them — to make room for her egg. Once the egg hatches, the young cuckoo is as ruthless as its mother. It pushes other eggs or babies over the edge of the nest so that it has the nest to itself. It even insists on being fed for a couple of weeks by the unlucky foster parents.

Did you know that...

- only *female* mosquitoes bite? They aren't looking for food for themselves; they're in search of a meal for their eggs. Blood contains special proteins that their eggs need to develop.

OUCH!

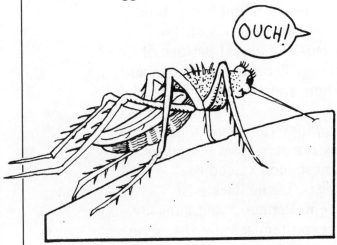

- the gastric-brooding frog of Australia swallows her eggs after she lays them? The eggs hatch inside the mother's stomach, and the tiny frogs climb out through her mouth.

- birds cheep inside their eggs when they are about to hatch, and crocodiles bark? When the babies of the Nile crocodile are big enough, they break into the air sac at the end of the eggs and start barking. That's to signal their mother to come dig the eggs out of the mud and break open the shells. She then carries the babies in her mouth to the river for their first swim.

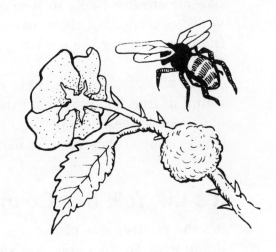

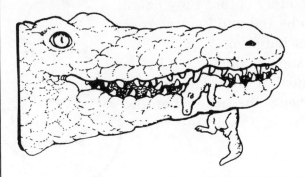

- some insects even get plants to take care of their eggs? The gall wasp lays its egg inside the growing leaf bud of trees or plants in the spring. As the plant keeps growing, it also grows a special cocoon-like case, called a gall, around the insect's egg. Look for them on tree branches.

Types of birds' eggs

There are more than 8000 species of birds in the world. As you might guess, their eggs vary a great deal in colour, shape and size.

Many birds lay eggs that are coloured and patterned to blend in perfectly with the surroundings. Ground layers tend to lay eggs with spots and streaks, so that it's difficult for hungry snakes and frogs to spot them. The actual pattern of spots or speckles is unique to each egg. Parents can recognize their own eggs even in a colony where there are hundreds of almost identical eggs.

Some birds, such as woodpeckers, hide their eggs in deep tree holes and burrows, where they are safe from predators. Birds that lay their eggs in hidden nests don't need to camouflage them. They lay white eggs. In the dark nest, parents are less likely to step on them. Penguins and gulls lay white eggs too, but these parents keep them safe by sitting on them or covering them with grass when the adults look for food.

Not all eggs are oval. Owls' eggs are quite round and are found in tree hollows. Seabirds lay eggs with tapered ends on bare rock ledges. The pointed end makes the eggs roll in a small circle so they are less likely to fall off the cliff.

It's the Yolk that Counts

It's the relative size of the egg — and its yolk — that counts. Robin eggs, for example, are small. They don't contain enough yolk for the babies to develop completely before they hatch. The babies are helpless and need to be fed and kept warm by their parents for several weeks after hatching.

The eggs of some ground layers, such as ducks, tend to be large because they contain a great deal of yolk. The embryos *have* to develop quickly inside their eggs, because when the ducklings hatch they might need to escape their nest fast!

Big, Small and Strange Eggs

- Giant ostriches lay the biggest eggs of all birds, and tiny hummingbirds the smallest. But the hummingbird's eggs are really giants compared to the mother. Each egg weighs an eighth of the mother. Compare that to an ostrich egg, which weighs a mere fiftieth of its mother.

- The yellowhammer is a small bird that's sometimes called the writing master, because its egg is covered with marks that look like mysterious scribbled writing.

The Egg-Rolling Challenge

Challenge a friend to perform an impossible feat — to roll a hard-boiled chicken egg in a straight line. The winner gets to keep the egg.

Don't worry about losing the egg. Because it's narrower at one end, it will tend to roll in a circle. Many birds' eggs are oval like chicken eggs: the shape makes it possible for several to fit in a nest when the adult is sitting on them. Three or four eggs fit neatly together in a nest, with the narrower ends pointing towards the middle.

Master builders

Birds are the most famous builders of all. There are as many types of nests as there are birds. Many birds build their nests in trees safe from their predators, or use holes in trees. Some dig tunnels in river banks. Others that dwell near water — ducks or swans — build their nests in reeds or on small islands. Some seabirds lay their eggs on the narrow ledges of sea cliffs. Here are some fascinating nests found in the bird kingdom.

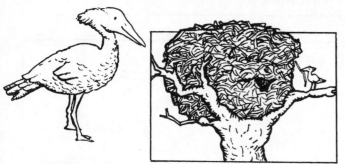

Built to Last

Africa's hammer-headed stork builds a mud-and-stick nest that has walls 1 metre (1 yard) thick. The nest is so strong that a grown man could walk around the top without breaking the walls.

Out of This World

Flamingos live in colonies and have a huge nesting ground where the birds gather to lay their eggs. The nesting ground looks like photographs of the moon's surface because the nests are mud cones shaped like craters.

Hothouse Nest

The male brush turkey builds a gigantic nest of mud and sticks. When the nest is finished, the male takes its temperature with his special bill. If the nest is too hot, he makes some openings to cool it down. If it's too cold, he may add some dirt for insulation.

Tree House Homes

Weaverbirds live in colonies and share an apartment-like nest. Between 20 and 50 pairs co-operate to build these enormous nests, which even have a waterproof domed roof. When done, the nests may measure 4.5 m (15 feet) by 3 m (10 feet), the size of a living-room! Each couple then builds its own apartment inside.

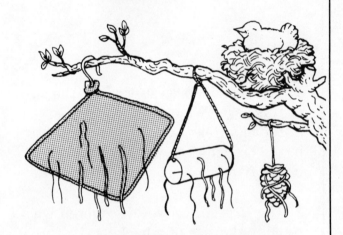

This Project is for the Birds

As the snow starts to melt and spring approaches, birds start to look for twigs or grass to build their nests. Sometimes they'll even borrow nesting material from people. One nest was made out of burnt matches and cigarette packages. Another nest was made entirely of watch springs. What country do you suppose that nest was found in?

You can invite more birds to nest in your neighbourhood by hanging out racks of nesting material.

You'll need:

string, yarn, ribbon or soft cloth
scissors
a toilet-paper roll or a coat hanger
    covered with an old pair of tights or
    a pine cone

1. Cut the string or yarn into pieces at least 10 cm (4 inches) long.

2. Punch holes in the toilet-paper roll or through the tights.
3. Thread the string or yarn through the holes or weave the string around the pine cone.
4. Hang the nest rack outside in a dry place before the snow melts. You might also want to add some moss, horsehair from an old sofa or fur from one of your pets.

Egg Olympics

Which bird takes the gold medal in these events? Answers on page 64.

1. The world's biggest eggs are the size of this page. Who lays them?
a. the albatross
b. the ostrich
c. the flamingo

2. The largest nest yet discovered was roughly the size of a back-yard swimming pool and weighed two tons — that's about as much as two small cars. Who built it?
a. crows
b. bald eagles
c. storks

3. The tiniest eggs are even smaller than your fingernail. Who lays them?
a. the canary
b. the swallow
c. the hummingbird

4. These eggs have the best shell costume. They are speckled and blend in so well with the surroundings that the judges can't see them. Who's the mother?
a. the robin
b. the owl
c. the sparrow

5. The mother of these eggs is the fastest hatcher. She sits on her eggs for only ten days. Who is she?
a. the great spotted woodpecker
b. the penguin
c. the chicken

Other Record Breakers

- The heaviest chicken egg on record weighed in at 450 g (16 ounces), eight times more than the average large egg. This heavyweight had a double yolk and a double shell.
- The toughest eggshell of all birds belongs to the ostrich. It's only as thick as the leather on a soccer ball, but you can stand on the egg without breaking the shell. It needs to be tough because it has to support its mother's weight of 18 kg (40 pounds) during incubation. By the way, it would take 45 minutes to cook one and you'd end up with enough egg-salad sandwiches to feed 24.

- The largest dinosaur egg in the world was found in southern France and was about the size of a beachball. It came from a dinosaur as long as a bus, which lived about 80 million years ago.
- The longest time eggs can last before hatching is 15 years. Crustacean eggs (such as brine shrimp) can hatch after lying this long in dry mud.
- The record for longest incubation period for birds is held by the albatross. It has an egg every other year, and the egg takes about 80 days to hatch.
- The highest number of yolks in a chicken egg was nine!

Why did the egg cross the road?

To get to the shell station!

3. Eating eggs

Did you eat an egg this morning? If you did, you carried on a very ancient tradition. Eggs have been eaten for breakfast for more than 100 000 000 years! Many dinosaurs, for example, were egg-eaters.

Most dinosaurs probably laid eggs like their modern-day relatives, the reptiles. We know that Protoceratops, a dinosaur with a bony ridge on the neck, laid eggs, because scientists discovered a fossilized nest of Protoceratops eggs. Can you guess what else they found in this nest? A fossilized skeleton of another dinosaur about the size of a dog. It was caught in the act of stealing an egg.

The tiny egg-stealing dinosaur was an oviraptor, which

means "egg thief." Oviraptors had no teeth so they couldn't eat meat; instead they sucked at eggs and fruit.

As soon as egg-laying animals began to appear on earth, egg-eating animals evolved, too. Here are a few examples.

In the ocean, the eggs of fish and many invertebrates (animals without backbones) are snapped up by other marine animals. They are often swallowed accidentally when fish take a large mouthful of something else. Fortunately, there are plenty of eggs to spare so that enough survive.

Everyone loves birds' eggs — mammals, reptiles and even other birds. Gulls and vultures are among the worst thieves. Gulls take eggs, then drop them on rocks so they will smash open. When vultures find thick-shelled ostrich eggs, they pelt them with stones to break them open. A vulture will sometimes grasp a stone in its beak and hammer an egg open, one of the few cases of a bird that uses a tool.

Although many snakes eat eggs, the egg-eating snake found in Africa and India hardly eats anything else. Its head and neck are only as wide as a grown-up's finger, and yet the snake can swallow a chicken's egg. To match this feat, you would have to swallow a whole pumpkin in one gulp.

How does this snake do it? The secret lies inside its jaws. First it gives a big yawn. Its special jaws unhinge, leaving an opening big enough for the whole egg to pass through. Inside the throat, 30 spiny bones that jut out of the backbone saw through the shell. When the shell collapses, the contents of the egg go into the snake's stomach. The snake spits out the shell's remains.

Humans eat many types of eggs: fish eggs called caviar or roe, turtles' eggs, and duck, goose and chicken eggs. Native people in Canada used to feed fish eggs to babies before cow's milk was available to them. The eggs were boiled and beaten until they were fluffy.

No wonder animals enjoy feasting on one another's eggs. Eggs are *designed* to be food, just like seeds and milk. Eggs store energy and nutrients for the embryo (the developing creature) inside. The embryo has all the food and water it needs to develop, just as you store all the food you need in a backpack when you go on a camping trip.

Eggs to the rescue

Eggs are nature's fast food, complete in their own packages. In fact, no fast food is richer in protein or cheaper to buy than eggs. One egg contains only 80 calories. Compare that to a hamburger with 240 calories, undressed! Besides, eggs are chock-full of the proteins, minerals and vitamins your body needs for growth and strength. Eggs are so rich in protein that nutritionists use them as a guide to measure the protein value of other foods. That's why *Dietary Guidelines for Americans* recommends that you make eggs a regular part of your diet.

We usually think of eggs as breakfast food, but eggs are often hidden ingredients in other foods. Without eggs, we wouldn't have waffles, mayonnaise, meatballs, cheesecake, ice cream, eggnog or birthday cakes. These are some of the jobs that eggs do in the kitchen:

Job	Foods
thicken	puddings, sauces, custards
make air bubbles	cakes, souffles, meringues
glue together	meatloaf, gravies, mayonnaise
garnish	soups, casseroles, salads

An Egg in Any Language

People have been eating chicken eggs for hundreds of years — scrambled or fried, devilled or poached. French and British cookbooks from 500 years ago even contain recipes for omelettes and custards. Here's how to write egg in different languages.

Egyptian hieroglyph:

Mandarin:

American
Sign Language:

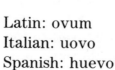

Latin: ovum
Italian: uovo
Spanish: huevo

Greek: αὐγό

French: oeuf
German: Eis
Punjabi:

Diner slang

Here's how waiters and waitresses translate your egg orders at a diner or greasy spoon. Can you figure them out? Answers on page 64.

1. Adam and Eve on a raft
2. Adam and Eve and wreck 'em
3. Two, sunny side up
4. One, over easy
5. Two, on a slice of squeal
6. Henberries

Fry an Egg on the Sidewalk

People sometimes complain that it's hot enough to fry an egg on the sidewalk. Egg whites begin to cook at about 63°C (145°F), yolks at a slightly lower temperature. On a really hot summer day, why not try to prove the saying true?

You'll need:

a piece of aluminum foil
some butter
one egg

1. Grease the aluminum foil with butter and place it on the sidewalk or on a hot rock.
2. Crack the egg open over the foil. Wait for it to cook.

Strange-but-true egg food

Suppose you open your lunchbox at school one day and find a weird-looking egg inside. It looks a bit like a hard-boiled egg, except the white isn't white at all — it's black. The yolk is full of brilliant blues and bright greens. Your friends don't think you should eat it, but you know this is a very special Chinese delicacy: a thousand-year-old egg.

Thousand-year eggs are very soft and creamy and taste a little bit like fish. They aren't really a thousand years old; they just look like they are. They aren't even cooked! To make them, raw goose eggs are covered in a thick layer of clay and left for six to eight weeks. Chemicals in the clay soak through the shell, hardening and preserving the egg inside.

Here are other faster and easier recipes to prepare. You probably have all the ingredients at home already, and you won't have to start two months in advance.

Egg Drop Soup (feeds 2)

a small bowl and fork
1 egg, beaten
1 can chicken broth
cooked rice, vegetables, or chicken if
    desired

1. Break an egg into a small bowl and beat thoroughly with a fork.
2. Prepare the chicken broth according to the directions on the can and bring it to a boil.
3. Add rice and other ingredients.
4. While the soup is boiling, pour in the beaten egg all at once and stir. The egg will form thin, noodle-like threads in the soup. Remove the broth immediately from the heat and serve.

Easy-Crust Pizza (8 slices)

a pizza pan
a mixing bowl
6 eggs
125 mL flour   ½ cup
2 mL salt   ½ tsp
2 mL oregano   ½ tsp
1 small can tomato or pizza sauce
250 mL sliced pepperoni   1 cup
125 mL chopped green pepper   ½ cup
1 medium tomato, sliced
125 mL shredded Cheddar cheese   ½ cup
250 mL shredded mozzarella   1 cup
    cheese

1. Preheat oven to 180°C (350°F).
Grease a 30-cm (12-inch) pizza pan.
2. In a medium-sized mixing bowl or
blender container, beat together the
eggs, flour, salt and oregano until they
are smooth. Pour this egg mixture
evenly onto the greased pan.
3. Bake about 15 to 20 minutes or until
the crust is firm and slightly golden.
4. Remove the pan from the oven.
Spread the sauce on the crust and top
with the remaining ingredients. Bake
the pizza for another 10 minutes at
180°C (350°F) or until the cheese has
melted.

German Egg Pancakes (feeds 1)

a large bowl
a frying pan
5 mL flour   1 tsp
10 mL milk   2 tsp
2 eggs
5 mL butter   1 tsp
5 mL sugar or your favourite jam   1 tsp
lemon wedge (optional)

1. In a large bowl, mix the flour and
milk to form a smooth paste.
2. Add the eggs and beat until the
batter is thoroughly mixed.
3. Heat the butter in a medium-sized
frying pan over medium heat. When
the butter starts to bubble, pour in the
batter. It should cover the entire pan.
4. Cook for four to five minutes, until
the top of the batter looks dry. Remove
from heat. Sprinkle the sugar evenly
over the entire pancake and squeeze
the lemon slice over the same area.
5. Lift half of the pancake with a
spatula and fold it over the other half.
6. Eat hot.

Guten Appetit!

Baked Alaska (makes 6)

You bake this ice-cream dessert in a hot oven. When served, it should be hot on the outside and cold inside. Why? The egg-white cover insulates the ice cream from the oven's heat.

a bowl
4 egg whites
2 mL salt   ½ tsp
125 mL sugar   ½ cup
6 graham crackers or soft cookies
6 scoops hard ice cream, well frozen

1. Preheat oven to 240°C (475°F).
2. To separate the yolks from the whites, crack the shell with a knife. Rock the yolk back and forth between the shell halves until all the white flows into a bowl. Save the yolks for cooking.

3. In a small bowl, beat the egg whites and salt until soft peaks form. Gradually add sugar a bit at a time and continue beating until stiff and glossy.

4. Top each cracker or cookie with ice cream and quickly cover with the egg meringue. Be sure to seal the edges completely. Swirl the top of the meringues into peaks.

5. Bake 2 to 4 minutes until meringue is delicately browned and serve.

Eggburger (feeds 1)

a frying pan
5 mL butter or margarine   1 tsp
1 egg
salt and pepper
chopped green pepper, salami or green
   onion (optional)
1 slice cheese (optional)
1 hamburger bun, heated or toasted

1. Melt butter in frying pan over
medium heat.
2. Break egg into pan. With a fork,
break the yolk and mix with the white.
Sprinkle with salt and pepper (and add
green pepper, salami or onions, if
desired). When egg is set, turn and
cook the other side.
3. Place cheese slice on warm bun and
cooked egg on top. Add your favourite
garnish — tomato slice, bacon, ketchup,
etc. — and eat at once.

Speedy Eggnog (one glass)

a blender
1 egg
1 tall glass of milk
5 mL honey or sugar, or scoop of   1 tsp
   ice cream
pinch of cinammon or nutmeg

1. Put the ingredients in a blender and
whip until frothy.
2. Make a fruitnog by using orange
juice instead of milk.

Mystery Egg Food

What popular sweet is made entirely of
egg whites and sugar? Need a hint? You
might toast one over the barbecue or
campfire.

4. The egg up close

Imagine that you are visiting a poultry farm that raises over 10 000 chickens. You bump into a chicken that's as big as a house. Surprised? You're in for another surprise when you spot one of the eggs laid by this giant. It's so big you could drive a small car into it. As you approach the egg, a door swings open and you climb in. The door silently swings closed.

Fortunately, the interior is light and airy so that you have no problem breathing or looking around. In fact, you can hear the clucking of chickens nearby and smell the grass in the fields. Suddenly you smell something awful! It has to be a skunk walking by.

Now how did the smell get in? At first glance the inner wall looks smooth, but when you examine it more closely, you can see it has a texture like an orange peel. The wall isn't solid either. It's filled with hundreds of tiny windows or pores, which let in air as well as sounds and smells. Each chicken eggshell has about 8000 pores in fact, and they are shaped like funnels with the widest part facing outwards. Their shape allows the oxygen to come in but makes it hard for the moisture from the yolk and white to escape.

What is the wall itself made of? If you guessed bone, you're close. The shell isn't exactly bone, but it's made up of the same material — calcium carbonate. This is the mineral that makes up animal bones and teeth.

When you reach up to touch the wall, the entire shell starts rolling and turning sideways. You have to walk quickly and

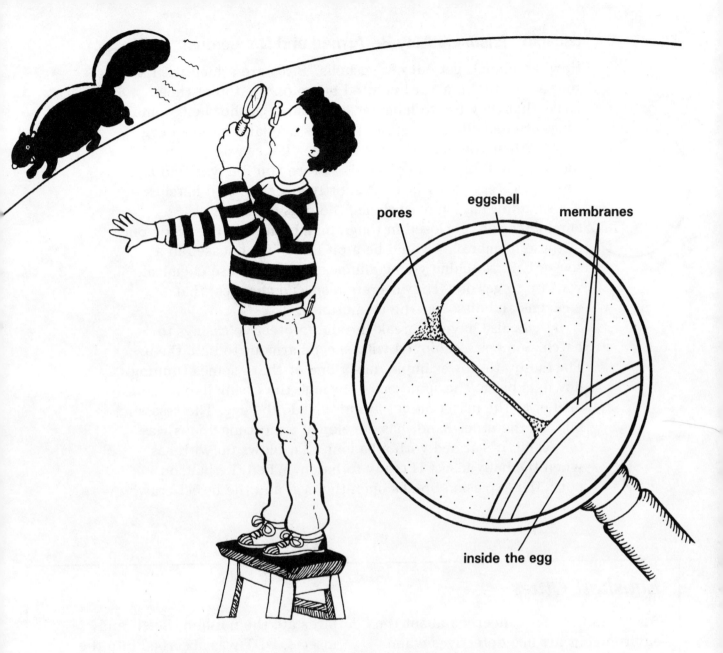

pores   eggshell   membranes

inside the egg

reach out to steady yourself with your hands. It's a bit like being in a huge tire that is slowly rolling forward. After a short while you feel dizzy because the egg seems to be rolling in a wide circle.

It's time to get out. Where's the door? It seems to have disappeared. You begin to knock hard against the wall with your fist, but it doesn't break. Thank heaven you've got a pencil in your pocket. You start to hammer at the wall with the pencil point and suddenly the shell cracks. Free at last!

Escaping Prisoners May Be Armed and Dangerous!

How do animals get out of eggshells? Birds are armed with a special egg tooth, a hard pointed bump on the top of their beaks that they use to hammer holes through the shell. Some types of crocodiles, turtles and snakes may also have an egg tooth. When you hear the expression, "It's as rare as a hen's tooth," you'll know the object is so rare you'll never find it. The chick's egg tooth falls off shortly after the bird hatches.

Instead of having hard shells, the eggs of fish and amphibians are enclosed in tough membranes. Being inside one of these membranes would be a bit like being encased in a soccer ball. Hatching young animals sometimes use chemical warfare to get out. They secrete a special chemical that weakens and dissolves the membranes.

Insects also have to break through protective casings to hatch. Some are equipped with special armour to help them. The mosquito, for example, has a line of sharp spines running down its back. The spines slice through the casing like a can opener as the insect moves around inside the egg. The assassin bug, on the other hand, has developed a most ingenious way to escape. It's armed with a balloon that blows up with gas when the baby insect is ready to hatch. When the balloon pops, the explosion breaks open the egg, and the insect crawls out.

Eggshell Clues

Scientists who are concerned about the environment act like detectives when they find birds' eggs. The important clues are found in the eggshells. Their chemical make-up helps the scientists to measure the effects of pollution on the food chain. For example, a chemical called DDT was once widely used to spray fields in order to kill the insects that attacked the crops. When birds ate the poisoned seeds and insects, DDT was absorbed into their bodies and affected their egg production; the eggshells were thinner and more fragile. They broke easily and fewer baby birds survived. By studying the eggshells, scientists determined that DDT was to blame. They argued that it could harm other living things too. DDT is now banned in Canada.

Egg Expressions

How strong is an eggshell?

Hold an egg in the palm of your hand and wrap your fingers around it. Now squeeze it over a bowl. You'll discover it doesn't break. Yet once an egg *has* cracked, it's very easy to crumble up the broken parts.

Both the calcium carbonate in the eggshell and its shape make the egg strong. This shape is called a dome. To see how strong domes really are, try this experiment.

Super Dome

The next time your family is having eggs for breakfast, ask if you can break the eggs.

1. Carefully crack open the eggs so that you have four equal halves. The best way to do this is by holding each egg sideways and neatly breaking it with a knife. Empty the contents into a bowl.
2. Place a book on top of the halves. Add a second book. Will the eggshells support a third one, too?

Try taping around the edge of the eggshells. Can they support more books now?

The eggshells can support the books because the weight doesn't press down on any single point. Instead, it travels down along the curved walls to the widest part of the dome. The weight is shared by all points around the base.

Man-made Eggshells

Have you ever been in a building whose roof is shaped like a dome? You might find this special structure in a church, planetarium or baseball stadium. The dome is one of the architect's favourite designs because it creates a spacious interior without the need for many supporting walls and pillars. In fact, the first planetarium ever built had a roof that copied the shape of an eggshell. It was constructed in Jenna, in Germany, in 1922.

If you cut across a dome horizontally (sideways), each slice would be a circular ring no matter where you cut. If you sliced it up and down like a loaf of bread, each slice would be an arch.

How Strong Is It?

Domes and arches are strong from the outside but weak from the inside. Try this strength test to see for yourself. You'll need nine rectangular blocks.
1. Use four blocks to build one set of stairs on the left and another four to make another set of stairs on the right. Have the two stairs meet and place the ninth block on the top.

2. Which is the easier way to make the arch collapse — by pressing down on the top block or by flipping the top one off with your finger from underneath?

It's harder to make the arch collapse by pressing down on the top block because the force is distributed down along the blocks. When you apply force from underneath, however, the arch easily comes apart. Similarly, an oval-shaped eggshell can support the entire weight of a parent bird without collapsing, but a fragile baby bird can break its way out from the inside — with the help of its special egg tooth.

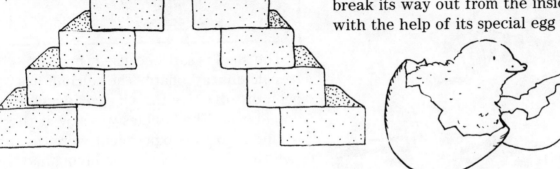

The disappearing eggshell

The eggshells of snakes and other reptiles, like lizards and newts, are soft, while those of birds are hard and brittle. Try this experiment to make a chicken eggshell soft, too.

You'll need:

a large glass
a raw egg
enough vinegar to fill the glass

1. Put the egg into the glass and place a spoon on it to weigh it down.

2. Fill the glass to the top with vinegar. Within minutes you'll see bubbles forming at the surface.

3. The next day gently lift the egg out of the glass. It will have become soft and rubbery. Maybe your friends will think it came from a snake. Some snakes' eggs are so strong they can bounce, but be careful with your egg. It's very weak now and will break if it's squeezed.

The shell is soft because it has lost its calcium carbonate. The calcium has been dissolved by the vinegar, which is a mild acid. The bubbles you saw at the beginning of the experiment were the sign that the process of dissolving had begun.

Eggshell Food for Plants

Many gardeners use eggshells to fertilize the soil. The calcium carbonate in the shells is good for the soil because it neutralizes some of the acids.

Geraniums, nasturtiums, morning glories, petunias, roses and tomatoes all need low-acid soil. If you have these plants in your garden, save eggshells in a plastic bag. When your plants need a snack, crumble up the shells with your fingers and sprinkle them around the stems of the plants.

Eggshell Plant Pots

You'll need:

half eggshells
potting soil
an egg carton
tomato, petunia or nasturtium seeds
a clear plastic bag and bag tie

1. Fill the eggshells with soil and place them in the carton.
2. Plant a couple of seeds in each pot and sprinkle them with water.

3. Cover the carton with the plastic bag to form a mini-greenhouse. Water droplets will collect on the inside of the bag, keeping the interior moist. Leave a small hole at the end of the bag to let the fresh air in.

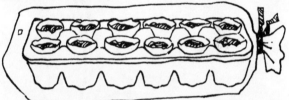

4. Put the carton beside a sunny window. When the seedlings are 6 or 7 cm (2 or 3 inches) high, poke some holes in the eggshells and plant them in larger flower pots or in the garden. As the eggshells decompose, they will fertilize the seedlings.

Inside the egg

Have you ever worried about the egg you just ate? Could it have turned into a chick if it hadn't been taken from the chicken? Probably not. Eggs destined for the kitchen usually aren't fertilized and cannot develop into chicks.

But if there's no chick, then what exactly *is* inside an egg? Take a look and see.

In a *fertilized* egg the yolk is the main food supply for a developing chick.

The eggshell is made mostly of calcium carbonate, which a developing embryo can use to form its bones. As the bones of the embryo get stronger, the eggshell gets weaker.

The inner and outer shell membranes are thin porous skins that help the egg "breathe" (oxygen passes in and carbon dioxide passes out). They also help to prevent the egg from drying out.

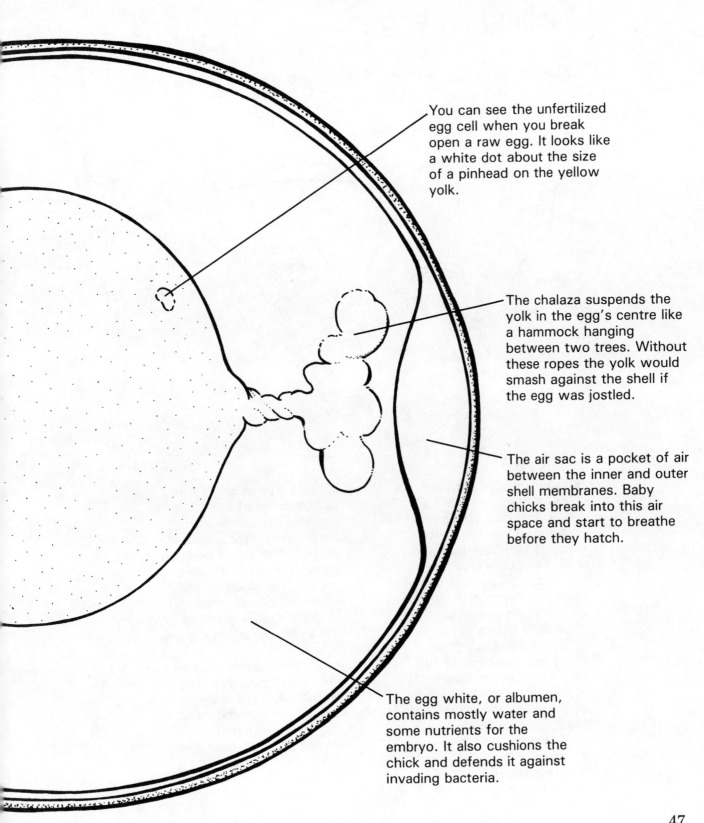

You can see the unfertilized egg cell when you break open a raw egg. It looks like a white dot about the size of a pinhead on the yellow yolk.

The chalaza suspends the yolk in the egg's centre like a hammock hanging between two trees. Without these ropes the yolk would smash against the shell if the egg was jostled.

The air sac is a pocket of air between the inner and outer shell membranes. Baby chicks break into this air space and start to breathe before they hatch.

The egg white, or albumen, contains mostly water and some nutrients for the embryo. It also cushions the chick and defends it against invading bacteria.

Making an egg

Here's how an egg is made, inside the body of a female chicken, or hen.

1. A hen is born with over 3500 tiny egg cells in her ovary. When she becomes an adult, these egg cells grow as each one forms a yolk. The ovary contains many egg cells with yolks at different stages of growth.

2. When the yolk is big enough, it enters the oviduct, a long tube that leads to the outside of the hen. Fertilization takes place at the top of the oviduct before either the white or the eggshell is formed.

3. Layers of egg white are wrapped around the yolk as it passes through the oviduct. The egg rotates as it moves, twisting up the thick strands of the chalazae. The inner and outer shell membranes are formed. The egg is pumped up with water and nutrients. Layers of shell are added in the lower end of the oviduct. Colour is added to the shell just before the egg is laid.

4. 24 hours after it leaves the ovary, the egg passes out of the hen's body through an opening called the cloaca. Almost immediately, another egg cell will be released from the ovary.

Once the egg is laid

After the fertilized egg is laid, it needs to be kept warm, or incubated, for the embryo to develop. Otherwise the embryo will die. As soon as a hen (or an incubator) provides that warmth, the embryo grows at an incredible speed. The tiny white speck becomes a fully formed chick in just 21 days!

Day 5

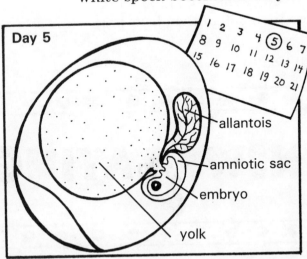

The embryo is protected inside the amniotic sac, which contains a watery fluid. A connecting membrane (the allantois) brings it oxygen and takes away wastes. Blood vessels branch out over the yolk to bring it food.

Day 15

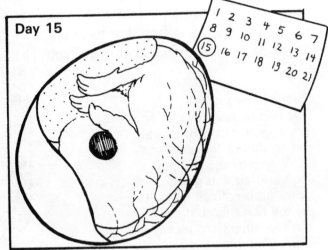

The chick now has feathers and is getting crowded. The allantois has grown all around the chick.

Day 20

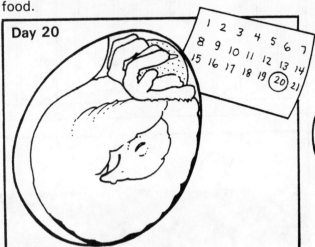

The chick has used up almost all the yolk and albumen (white). Soon it will break into the air space and begin breathing and peeping.

Day 21

The chick uses its egg tooth to hammer its way out of its shell.

49

From the farm to you

Years ago people used to keep a few chickens, ducks or geese to have a daily supply of fresh eggs. Nowadays people usually buy eggs at the store. Those eggs have come from a poultry farm, which may have more than 10 000 hens. Egg production is a major industry in America: more than 350 million hens produce 5 billion dozens of eggs.

Let's follow an egg from the hen to you.

Meet the Egg Layer
This hen usually lays an egg a day, or about 300 a year, and so do her three or four other cagemates. All the hens are fed and given water automatically. Don't tell the hen this, but she and the others are tricked into laying eggs almost every day. How? The light in the building is controlled to fool the hens into thinking it's springtime, their biggest egg-laying time.

How Many Eggs?

The number of eggs a bird lays depends on what kind of bird she is. Some species are determinant layers; others are indeterminant layers.

Determinant layers produce only a fixed number of eggs in a clutch even if something happens to one of the eggs. Other birds, like ducks and hens, are indeterminant layers. They can keep on laying to replace eggs that are lost.

Long ago farmers used to have fake nest eggs. They would put these eggs in the chicken coop or barn to persuade the hens to lay their eggs inside a clean spot rather than on the ground. Perhaps you've heard people say they have a nest egg. This means they've been saving money for a special project.

Today, at a modern poultry farm, eggs are removed each day so that the hens are tricked into producing another one.

Get Rolling!

The egg is collected automatically. It rolls out of the cage onto a conveyor belt that moves it along to a packing area. Here it is placed in an open carton called a flat, along with 29 other eggs. After a brief rest in a chilled room, it is carried onto a refrigerated truck and driven to a grading station. What happens in the grading station? Turn the page to find out.

COOLER ROOM

Don't Judge an Egg By Its Colour

Myth 1. Brown eggs are healthier for you than white eggs.
False. Shell colour has no effect on the taste or food quality of chicken eggs. Different breeds of hens lay different coloured eggs — even blue.
Myth 2. Pale yolks are not as nutritious or fresh as dark yellow or orange yolks.

False. The hen's diet determines the yolk's colour. Hens that eat wheat lay eggs with light yellow yolks. Hens fed corn or alfalfa have darker yellow yolks.

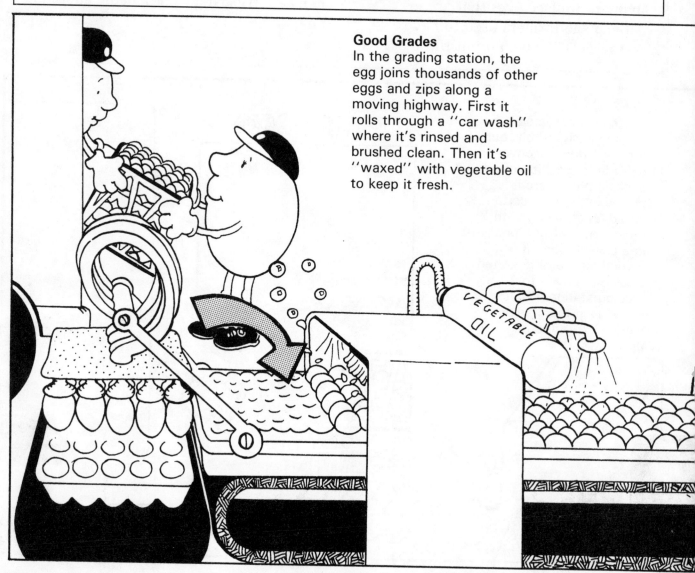

Good Grades
In the grading station, the egg joins thousands of other eggs and zips along a moving highway. First it rolls through a "car wash" where it's rinsed and brushed clean. Then it's "waxed" with vegetable oil to keep it fresh.

The Two-Second Freshness Test

How can you tell whether one egg is fresh and another is old? Put them both in water and observe which one floats higher. The higher floater will be the older egg. It has a larger air sac than the fresh egg because its yolk and white have started to dry up. Cook it first!

Next it passes its first test, which is called candling because the process used to be done with candles. As it passes over a strong light, any cracks and imperfections become visible.

If it gets a high score in quality, the egg will receive a grade A and be packed in a carton marked either extra large, large, medium, small or peewee, depending on its weight.

Then it's sent to the cooler to wait for the trucks that will take it to the store. If it's judged second-best, it gets a grade B and may be sent to the store or a food-processing factory. But what if it fails all the tests and gets a C? It will never be sent to the store. Instead, it'll be turned into dried-egg powder or canned as a liquid and eventually be used to make noodles, cake mixes, shampoos or adhesives.

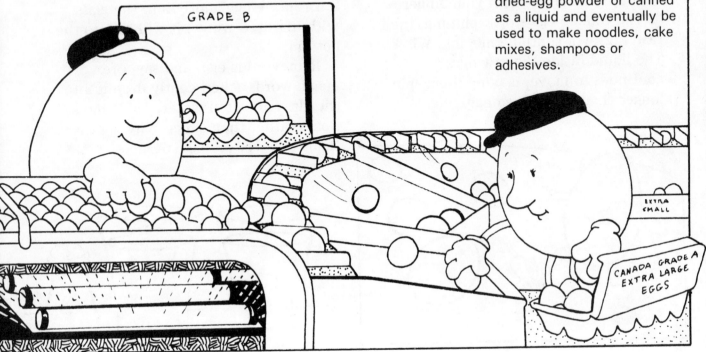

5. Egg fun

Be your own magician and astound your friends
with these three tricks.

Find the Hard-boiled Egg

Challenge your friends to find the hard-
boiled egg on the plate without
cracking any of them.

You'll need:

5 raw eggs
1 hard-boiled egg in its shell

1. Put each egg on the table and spin it
on its side.
2. Stop the egg from spinning by
quickly touching it with your finger.
3. The cooked egg stops spinning; the
raw eggs will continue moving. Why?
The liquid inside the raw eggs
continues to move, making them spin
longer than the cooked egg.

Make It Float

Can your friends explain why an egg
suddenly floats?

You'll need:

2 large glasses of luke-warm water
75 mL salt   ⅓ cup
1 fresh egg

1. Shortly before you perform this
trick, pour the salt into one glass and
stir until the salt has dissolved.
2. Drop the egg gently into the glass
with unsalted water. It will sink to the
bottom.
3. Remove this egg, and say a few
magic words. Then gently drop it into
the glass of salted water. This time it
floats rather than sinks. Why does it
float? Answer on page 64.

Egg Physics

Challenge a friend to push a shelled hard-boiled egg into a narrow-necked bottle without damaging the egg. Ask a grown-up to stand by during your performance because you have to drop a burning piece of paper into the bottle.

You'll need:

cooking oil, butter or margarine
a 225-mL glass baby bottle   8-ounce
3 or 4 small shelled hard-boiled eggs
a strip of paper, 10 cm (4 inches) long
   by 10 cm (4 inches) wide

1. Put some cooking oil, butter or margarine around the mouth of the bottle.
2. Place the egg on the mouth of the bottle and challenge your friend to push it inside without breaking it.

3. When he gives up, it's time to act as the magician. Fold the paper to form an accordion. Light one end with a match and drop it into the bottle.

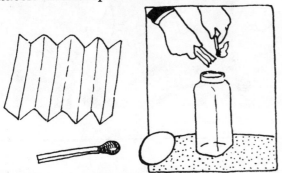

4. Now quickly place the egg over the mouth of the bottle. It will be sucked into the bottle. (The burning paper has heated the air inside the bottle so that the air has expanded. When the paper stops burning, the air cools and contracts again. This creates a vacuum that will suck the egg into the bottle.)

5. Challenge your friend to get the egg out. When he's given up, invert the bottle so that the egg drops down into the neck. Hold the bottle to your lips and blow a fast, hard blast of air into the bottle. The egg will zoom out, so get ready to catch it. (The egg acts as a valve that opens while you're blowing air into the bottle and then closes when you stop. The extra air is trapped inside, behind the egg, when the valve suddenly closes. That pressure forces the egg out.)

WARNING:

Be sure to practise Step 4 *before* you perform it in front of an audience. Experiment to see how long you should let the paper burn inside the bottle before you put the egg over the mouth. If the air inside gets too hot, the egg will be sucked into the bottle too suddenly and may break.

Three great egg-carton games

For all three of these games, you'll need an egg board. Here's how to make one.

Making the Egg Board

You'll need:

6 egg cartons
scissors and tape

1. Cut the covers off three egg cartons and tape the bottoms together side by side.

2. Now you have to cut out 36 cups from the other three cartons to make caps. You'll need these caps to cover the holes in the egg board.

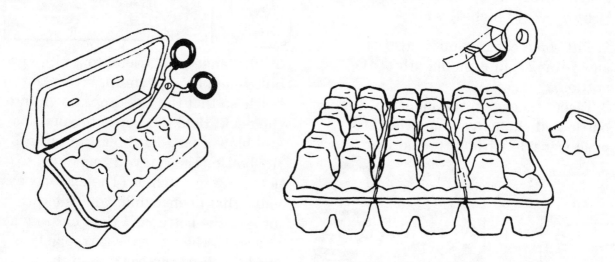

What do you call a bird that's afraid of its shadow?

Chicken!

The Amazing Maze

This game is for two players. One person sets up the maze and the other tries to discover where the hidden path is.

You'll need:

1 egg board
36 caps
30 small markers (buttons, marbles, beans)

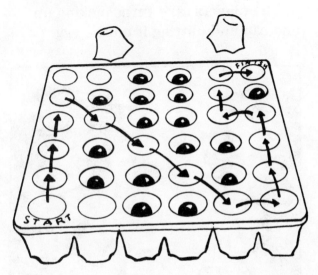

1. Prepare your egg board as shown on page 56. Label the bottom left cup START and the top right cup FINISH.
2. Place the markers in some of the cups on the board, taking care to leave a path of empty cups from START to FINISH. You can put in a few dead ends, too.
3. To hide the paths, cover all the bottom cups with the 36 individual caps.

4. Beginning at START, a player removes one cap at a time trying to find the hidden trail. If the cup is empty, the player has a second turn and can remove another cap. But if the cup contains a marker, he or she must replace all the caps, return to START and begin again. Players must remember which cups are empty.
5. When the first player reaches the end, he or she prepares another maze for the second player to discover.

Concentration

To play this game, you have to concentrate to remember where the markers are hidden, just like the games where sets of pictures are hidden.

You'll need:

1 egg board
36 caps
18 **pairs** of markers (small enough to put in the cups)

1. Set up the egg board as shown on page 56.

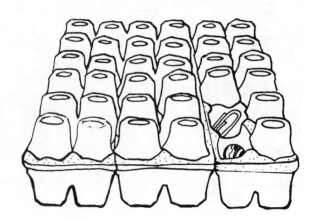

2. Put the pairs of markers in the empty cups on the egg board. Mix up the pairs so that they will be hard to find.
3. Cover them with the caps.
4. Each player is allowed to remove two caps at a time. If she finds a matching set of markers, she takes them out and gets a second turn. If the markers don't match, she puts the cups back and the next player has a turn.
5. Whoever gets the most pairs of markers wins the game.

S.O.S.

This is a variation of tic-tac-toe and requires two players.

You'll need:

an egg board
36 caps

1. Mark 18 caps with S and the other 18 with O.
2. Put all the caps in a pile on the table.
3. The players take turns picking up one cap and putting it on the egg board.

4. The goal is to complete an S.O.S. in a vertical, horizontal or diagonal line. Score one point for each S.O.S. or two points if you complete two intersecting S.O.S's in the same turn.

Egg art

Before oil paints were invented in the fifteenth century, egg yolks were an important ingredient in paint. Artists mixed their pigments, or powdered colours, with an egg yolk to bind the powder together and help make the paint stick to the canvas or wood they were painting on. This technique, called egg tempera, enabled them to build up many layers of paint and to put in incredible detail. But they had to work fast! Egg tempera paint dried very quickly. Artists switched over to oil paints because they dried more slowly.

Preserve Your Pictures

Here's how to make your artwork more permanent.

You'll need:

1 egg yolk
a cup
a pin
tempera paint, pastels or chalk
manila paper
paint brush
small cup or bowl

1. Separate the yolk from the white (see step 2 on page 36).
2. Hold the yolk over a small cup and poke a small hole in the membrane so that the yolk pours into the cup. Throw out the membrane.

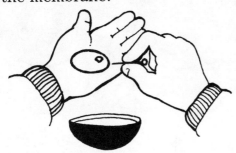

3. Make your drawing or painting, then carefully brush a thin layer of egg yolk over your picture. The yolk will glue the chalk or paint to the paper and also give a slight glaze, or shine, to the work.

Try another technique: brush on the egg yolk first, then do your drawing or painting. What happens?

If you think of decorating eggs only at Easter, think again.
You can use eggs for celebrations throughout the year!

Papier-Mâché Valentines

You'll need:

2 sheets of newspaper
2 half eggshells and one whole shell
tape
scissors and glue or paste

1. Follow the instructions in the box on page 61 and blow out the insides of the eggs.
2. Cut the newspaper into thin strips about 2.5 cm (1 inch) wide.
3. Tape the half eggshells to the whole egg to form a heart shape.

4. Dip strips into the paste and use them to glue everything together. Smooth strips over the entire structure, overlapping them to make it strong.

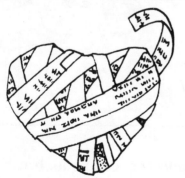

5. Let this papier-mâché layer dry for a few hours, then do another layer. Paint on your own design, when everything is dry.

Finger Puppets

Use the same papier-mâché technique to make a puppet's head. Pieces of yarn or material can be used for hair.

Christmas Decorations

Decorated eggs can make unusual tree ornaments. Start by blowing the insides out of a raw egg. See the box for how to do this. Tie a match onto the end of piece of wool and insert it into the hole of the eggshell. That will anchor the eggshell when you hang it on the tree.

If you have a dozen or more decorated eggs, thread them together using a bright piece of wool to make an egg chain. Drape it across the window or on the tree.

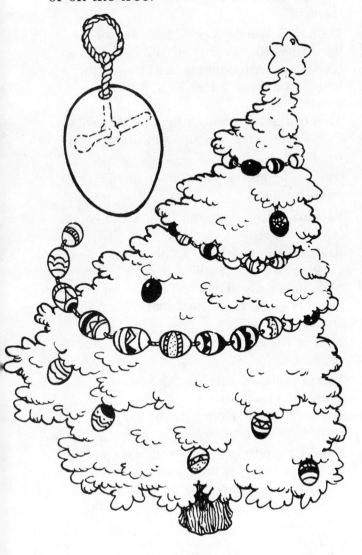

How to blow out the contents of an egg

You'll need:

an egg
a safety pin or nail
a small container with a lid

1. With a safety pin or a small nail, poke a hole through the top and bottom of the egg, and inside to break the membrane. Make the hole slightly larger in the broad end.

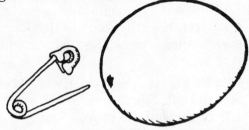

2. Hold the egg over a container. Now blow through the hole at the top. Keep your mouth closed around the hole so that no air escapes. (If nothing happens, you need to make the holes slightly bigger.)

3. Once all the yolk and white have dropped into the container, put the lid on and place it in the refrigerator. You can use the egg to make eggnog or for cooking.

Glossary

Amphibians Cold-blooded animals with backbones that spend part of their life on water and part on land. They must lay their eggs in water. Examples: frogs, newts, salamanders.

Birds Warm-blooded animals with backbones that have wings and feathers and breathe air using lungs. Birds must incubate their eggs so they will hatch.

Clutch A set number of eggs laid by each bird; the number varies from one species to another. Examples: robins lay 3 to 5 eggs and loons lay 2 eggs.

Cold-blooded animals Animals whose temperature is the same as their surroundings. Examples: fish, amphibians, reptiles.

Egg The female reproductive cell before it is fertilized. Egg also means the place where the embryo develops; it has either a soft or a hard shell.

Embryo The baby animal that develops inside the egg or the body after the egg is fertilized. Embryos that grow inside eggs absorb food from the yolk, while embryos that develop within the mother's womb get their food and oxygen from the mother's blood.

Fertilization This occurs whenever a sperm supplied by the father and an egg cell supplied by the mother join to make a fertilized egg, which then develops into a baby animal.

Incubate To keep the eggs at a favourable temperature so they will hatch. If birds didn't keep their eggs warm, the embryos inside would lose their body heat and die. Cold-blooded animals don't usually incubate their eggs.

Insects Creatures without backbones, whose bodies are protected by a hard covering (exoskeleton) and divided into three segments. Insects usually have three pairs of legs and two pairs of wings. Many insects lay their eggs on or near a food supply so the larvae will have enough to eat.

Instinct Inborn behaviour shown by an animal when it responds to its environment. For example, many birds instinctively build nests before they lay their eggs.

Larvae Young animals (caterpillars, silk worms, tadpoles) that look quite different from their parents. They pass through several stages in their life cycle before becoming adults; the larval stage is one of them.

Mammals Warm-blooded animals with backbones that bear their young alive and feed them with milk made in the mother's body. Examples: mice, dogs, humans, whales.

Membrane A thin, soft flexible layer of tissue protecting an egg or an organ inside the body.

Ovary The part of the female animal that produces eggs.

Predator An animal that hunts and eats other animals.

Reptiles Cold-blooded animals with backbones that breathe air using lungs, have dry, scaly skins, and lay white, leathery eggs. Examples: snakes, lizards, crocodiles.

Sperm The reproductive cell produced by the father.

Warm-blooded animals Animals (birds, mammals) that have a high body temperature that remains the same regardless of the climate.

Yolk A round mass of semi-liquid egg food for the developing embryo. Bird and reptile eggs have a large supply of yolk; marine eggs have a small supply and hatch as larvae.

Index

Air sac, 23, 46, 53
Albatross, 29
Amphibians, 15, 40
   See also individual species
Ants, 22
Aphids, 22
Assassin bug, 40

Baked Alaska, 36
Birds
   eggs, 4, 15, 23-25, 28,
     31, 38-40, 42, 46, 47
   See also various species,
     Chickens' eggs, Clutch
   nests, 21, 22, 26, 27, 28, 49
   types of layers, 51
Brush turkey, 26

Candling, 52
Chalaza(e), 47, 48, 49
Chickens (or hens), 48, 49, 50,
   51, 52
Chickens' eggs, 9, 16, 19, 25,
   29, 38, 39, 40, 46-49, 53
   See also Egg production,
     Poultry farm
Clutch, 51
Cold-blooded animals, 15
   See also Amphibians, Fish,
     Reptiles
Crocodiles, 6, 23, 40
Cuckoos, 22

DDT, 40
Domes, 42-43
Dietary Guidelines for Amer-
   icans, 32
Dinosaurs, 29, 30, 31
Dyeing eggs, 12, 13
Ducks, 24, 51

Eagles, 28
Easter, 9-13, 60, 61
Easy-Crust Pizza, 35
Eggburger, 37
Egg cartons, 56-58
Egg chain, 61
Egg Drop Soup, 34
Egg-eating snake, 31
Egg expressions, 32, 33, 40
Eggnog, 37, 61
Egg production, 50, 51
Egg sacs, 20

Eggshells, 4, 9, 14, 15, 20, 29,
   39-43, 47, 48, 52
Egg tempera, 59
Egg tooth, 40, 43
Egg white (or albumen), 33,
   37, 47, 48, 49, 61
Embryos, 14, 15, 16, 24, 31,
   47, 49
Evil Eye, 9
Evolution, 14, 15

Farmers, 8, 9, 51
   See also Poultry farm, Egg
     production
Fertility customs, 8
Fertilization, 14, 18, 48
Fertilizer, eggshell, 45
Fish eggs, 4, 16, 17, 19, 31, 40
Flamingos, 4
Fly, African, 22
Frogs, 4, 17, 19, 23

Gall wasp, 23
Games, 11, 56-58
Geese, 31, 34
German Egg Pancakes, 35
Grading station, 51, 52
Gulls, 31

Hammer-headed storks, 26
Hornbills, 21
Hummingbirds, 4, 25, 28

Incubation, 21, 28, 29, 49
Insects' eggs, 4, 15, 17, 22,
   23, 40
   See also Ants, Assassin
     bugs, Fly, Mosquitoes

Krashanka eggs, 8

Larvae, 14, 15
Legends and myths, 6-9
Lizards, 44

Magic tricks, 54, 55
Mammals, 15, 31
Marine animals, 4, 14, 15, 16,
   17, 18
Membranes, 14, 20, 40, 46, 47
Mosquitoes, 17, 23, 40
Mussels, 16

Nest eggs, 51

Nests, 21, 22, 26, 27, 28, 49
Nest rack, 27
Newts, 44

Octopus, 4, 18
Ostriches, 4, 25, 29, 31
Oviraptors, 18
Owls, 24
Oysters, 18

Paradise fish, 19
Parents, care of eggs, 17-24
   See also Reproduction
Passover, 10, 11
Penguins, 24
Poultry farm, 50, 51
Predators, 17, 19, 30, 31
Protoceratops, 30
Pysanky eggs, 13
Pythons, 15
   See also Snakes
Puppets, finger, 50

Recipes
   Baked Alaska, 36
   Egg Drop Soup, 34
   Easy-Crust Pizza, 35
   Eggburger, 37
   German Egg Pancakes, 35
   Speedy Eggnog, 37
Reptiles' eggs, 4, 15, 20, 31,
   44
   See also Crocodiles,
     Lizards, Newts,
     Salamanders, Snakes,
     Turtles
Reproduction, 14
Rheas, 21
Robins, 4, 24

Salamanders, 17
Sea horses, 4, 18
Snakes, 4, 6, 15, 20, 31, 40,
   41
Spiders, 4, 20
Superstitions, 9

Thousand-year-old eggs, 34
Toads, 17, 20
Turtles, 20, 31, 40

Ukrainian, 8, 13
   See also Farmers

Weaverbirds, 25
Witches, 9

Vultures, 31

Yolks, 14, 24, 33, 46, 47, 48,
   49, 52, 59
   painting with, 59
   separating from whites, 36

Answers:

Egg Olympics, page 28
1. b. ostrich
2. b. bald eagles
3. c. hummingbird
4. c. sparrow
5. a. great spotted
   woodpecker

Diner slang, page 33
1. Two eggs on toast
2. Two scrambled eggs on
   toast
3. Two fried eggs, yolks up
4. One fried egg, flipped
   over
5. Two eggs on fried ham
6. Eggs

Make It Float, page 54
It floats for the same reason
it's easier to swim in the
ocean than in a lake or pool.
The salt water makes you
buoyant because you are
less dense than water.

ALSO IN THIS SERIES:

The Amazing Apple Book
Paulette Bourgeois
Illustrations by Linda Hendry

ISBN 0-201-52334-5

COMING SOON:

The Amazing Paper Book
Paulette Bourgeois
Illustrations by Linda Hendry

ISBN 0-201-52377-9

Addison-Wesley Publishing Company, Inc.
Route 128
Reading, Massachusetts 01867